This Journal Belongs to:

👤 _____

📞 _____

📍 _____

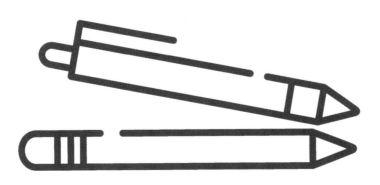

WRITING PROMPTS FOR MIDDLE SCHOOL

First paperback edition February 2022

ISBN: 9798423943875

Published by Rita SKPress

ABOUT THIS BOOK:

Writing is used as a tool to help middle school students prepare for the high school experience.

This workbook is created to help middle school students expand their writing and critical thinking skills with this list of more than 10 unique topics!

There are ten topics to write about: fun, reflective, creative, argumentative, persuasive, narrative, short story, imaginative, science, and expository.

These prompts are aimed at middle school students but younger or older writers might enjoy trying them as well.

Have fun, imagine, explore, and start writing!

TABLE OF CONTENT:

Your teacher walks into the classroom with feathers like a duck and the head of a chimpanzee. You may not laugh; if you do, you will be sent to the principal's office. What do you do to avoid laughing?

....

....

....

....

....

....

....

You wake up one morning with ears and a tail like a donkey. What happens next?

....

....

....

....

....

....

....

A lobster is your substitute teacher; what happens next?

....

....

....

....

....

....

....

....

Someone replaced your favorite lunch with the most disgusting lunch, which they dare you to eat. Describe the food and will you eat it?

....

....

....

....

....

....

If you could talk to a wild animal, what would you talk about?

....

....

....

....

....

....

....

You walk in the woods, and a skunk sees you and invites you to a party. What happens next?

....

....

....

....

....

....

....

....

The teacher welcomes a new student into the class. Every time you look at the new student, they make a funny animal noise. Describe the noise and what happens next.

....

....

....

....

....

....

You are the only one that can smell outer space. Describe the smell to your best friend.

....

....

....

....

....

....

....

....

The teacher announces that you are going to learn new communication skills using your toes. Explain how it works.

....

....

....

....

....

....

....

Write a thank-you letter to your best friend who gave you a piece of gum that smells like trash and tastes like Brussel sprouts.

....

....

....

....

....

....

....

My family forgot that they left me at the airport. They boarded the plane while I was waiting in the boarding area. Describe what happens next

....

....

....

....

....

....

....

Describe a world that is ruled by animals

....

....

....

....

....

....

....

....

....

Describe an inside joke that only your friends and family know about.

....
....
....
....
....
....

Create new rules for your school. What would it be?

....
....
....
....
....
....
....
....

Write about the funniest holiday you have ever been on.

....

....

....

....

....

....

....

....

Write about the funniest incident you have ever experienced.

....

....

....

....

....

....

....

....

What was the best joke that you heard during the last week? What made that joke so funny to you?

....

....

....

....

....

....

....

Pretend that you are going to be performing a stand-up comedy act for your friends and family members. Write a draft of what your act might sound like.

....

....

....

....

....

....

....

Write a list of funny excuses that you could use to get out of doing your homework.

....

....

....

....

....

....

....

Pretend that you are creating a holiday dedicated entirely to humor. How would you celebrate this day?

....

....

....

....

....

....

....

....

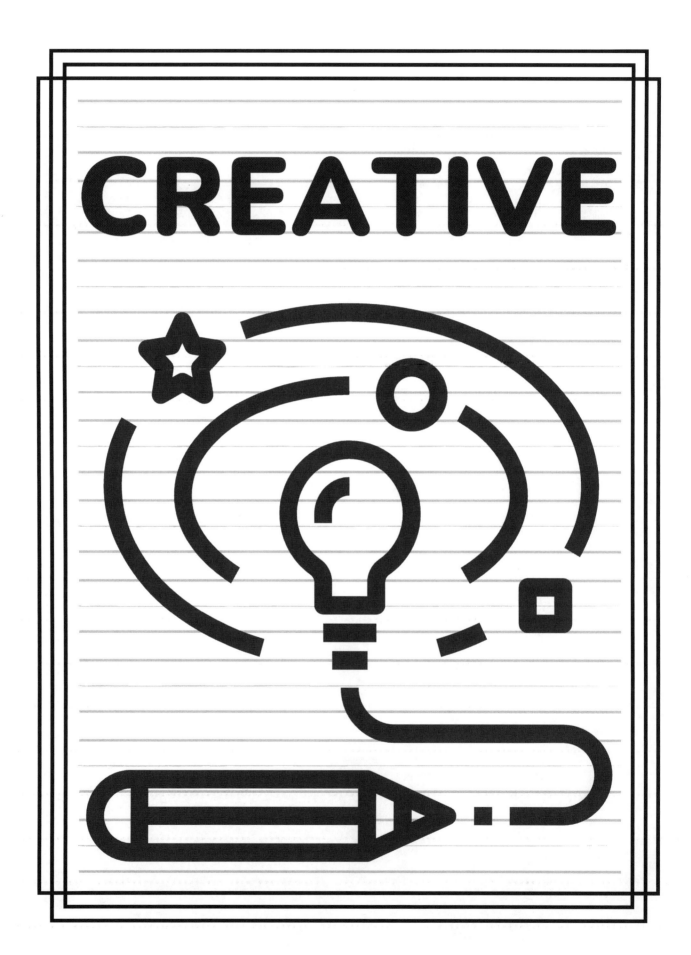

How did you show kindness to someone else today?

....

....

....

....

....

....

From a scale of 1 to 10 how would you describe your day? 10 being amazing and 1 being very bad.

....

....

....

....

....

....

....

....

....

Did you read or see anything that made you upset?

....

....

....

....

....

....

....

Write about your favorite childhood toy

....

....

....

....

....

....

....

....

Write a thank-you note to someone who deserves it

....

....

....

....

....

....

....

....

Write an apology note to someone you should say sorry too.

....

....

....

....

....

....

....

....

Create new food you believe people will like it. What would you name it? How will it taste? What ingredients would you put inside it?

....

....

....

....

....

....

Invent a new drink. What would you name it? How will it taste? What ingredient would you put inside it?

....

....

....

....

....

....

....

....

Create a new superhero. What are the powers? What will it look like?

....

....

....

....

....

....

....

Describe what your country will look like 10 years from now.

....

....

....

....

....

....

....

....

What does it mean to be successful?

....

....

....

....

....

....

....

....

If you can redecorate your room what will it look like?

....

....

....

....

....

....

....

....

What does your dream house look like?

....

....

....

....

....

....

....

....

Is it possible to be happy without money? How?

....

....

....

....

....

....

....

....

How has math contributed to a modern technological device?

....

....

....

....

....

....

....

Describe three skills you are good at and three skills you would like to improve or have?

....

....

....

....

....

....

....

....

What would you do if you were the school principal?

....

....

....

....

....

....

....

....

....

....

....

....

....

....

....

....

REFLECTIVE

Describe the events in your day over the course of a week. Which day was the busiest? Did it feel that way?

....

....

....

....

....

....

....

Reflect on your relationship with someone in your family. How do you get along with them? What would you change about your behavior? What could they change?

....

....

....

....

....

....

....

Record your emotional reactions for several days in a row. Do you see a pattern? What can you do to change an emotional pattern?

Make a goal in the morning and reflect back on it at night. Write about whether you accomplished that goal, and if so, what helped you. If you didn't accomplish your goal, reflect on what you could do differently next time.

List your goals and priorities for the week. Reflect on whether they reflect your personality or just your schedule.

....

....

....

....

....

....

....

....

....

....

....

....

....

....

....

....

Describe your favorite things about yourself. What makes you unique? What makes you belong to a bigger group, such as your family, friends, or community?

....

....

....

....

....

....

....

....

....

....

....

....

....

....

....

Do you have skills that you feel make you stand out? Do you use these skills enough in your life?

....

....

....

....

....

....

....

....

What things are you look forward to?

....

....

....

....

....

....

....

....

What things have surprised you about life in general?

....

....

....

....

....

....

....

....

What things in life scare you?

....

....

....

....

....

....

....

....

What things are you most grateful for in your life?

....

....

....

....

....

....

....

....

In what ways have you changed from the person you were five or ten years ago?

....

....

....

....

....

....

....

....

Are there things in your life you need to let go of? What are they?

....

....

....

....

....

....

....

What qualities do you look for when choosing your friends?

....

....

....

....

....

....

....

....

What things make you feel the most energized?

....

....

....

....

....

....

....

....

What do you love the most about your favorite hobbies? Are there ways to incorporate that into other areas of your life?

....

....

....

....

....

....

....

When we reflect upon our childhood, we often come back to a few key events that had a major impact on us. Write about one of those defining events from your childhood.

....

....

....

....

....

....

....

....

....

....

....

....

....

....

ARGUMENTATIVE

Should students have a greater say in what they learn? Why?

....

....

....

....

....

....

....

Is it ever fair for minorities to receive special treatment or consideration? why?

....

....

....

....

....

....

....

Do girls or boys face more societal pressure or do they face equal amounts?

....

....

....

....

....

....

....

Does reality television accurately depict real life? Do movies?

....

....

....

....

....

....

Do athletes, celebrities, and CEOs deserve to make more money than the average person?

....

....

....

....

....

....

....

....

What responsibilities do people have to help one another out?

....

....

....

....

....

....

....

Should parents monitor their children's Internet and/or social media usage?

....

....

....

....

....

When it comes to government monitoring, which is more important-individual privacy or national security?

....

....

....

....

....

How does the location someone grows up in affect who they become?

....

....

....

....

Do participation trophies have value or do they undervalue the achievements of the winners?

....

....

....

....

....

Is climate change real, and is it happening?

....

....

....

....

Should religion be kept out of politics or brought into it?

....

....

....

....

Is it immoral to download copyrighted content illegally or is it something that is a violation of the law, but not an issue of ethics?

....

....

....

....

....

Should gym class (physical education) be required in school for all students?

....

....

....

....

....

Should students be allowed to use phones in class?

....

....

....

....

Should there be a legal age limit for social media?

....

....

....

....

....

....

Should there be a school voucher system?

....

....

....

....

....

Should teachers accept late work?

....

....

....

....

....

Are electric cars as environmentally friendly as they claim to be?

....

....

....

....

....

....

Is animal testing for pharmaceuticals necessary?

....

....

....

....

....

What is the biggest problem facing your generation?

....

....

....

....

PERSUASIVE

What are the benefits or detriments of a single-gender education?

....

....

....

....

....

....

Is learning a second language beneficial or a waste of time? Why?

....

....

....

....

....

Should student textbooks be replaced by Chromebooks? Why?

....

....

....

....

....

Are they an important and necessary part of the educational experience?

....

....

....

....

....

....

Should college athletes be payed for playing?

....

....

....

....

....

Should females be allowed to play football? Why?

....

....

....

....

....

Is having a job in middle or high school a good idea? Why?

....

....

....

....

....

....

Should teens be allowed to vote?

....

....

....

....

....

Should this country change its immigration policies?

....

....

....

....

Should there be tougher federal restrictions for content on the Internet?

....

....

....

....

....

....

Write a letter to the editor about an article in the paper with which you agree or disagree.

....

....

....

....

....

Do you believe that smokers should be able to smoke wherever they want?

....

....

....

....

....

The best thing about middle school is...

....

....

....

....

....

....

The worst thing about middle school is...

....

....

....

....

Would you rather shrink to the size of a penny or grow to the size of a building?

....

....

....

....

....

Children watch too much television. Do you agree?
Take a stand and support it. Convince your reader of
your position.

....

....

....

....

....

why or why not uniforms should or should not be
required in your school?

....

....

....

....

Convince your friend to swap their packed lunch with
yours.

....

....

....

....

....

Vandalism is becoming a problem in today's society. Do you think teenagers who vandalized should pay fines or serve mandatory community service to help repair the damage? Write an essay to convince people of your position.

....

....

....

....

....

....

....

....

....

....

....

....

....

....

....

Your principal wants to invite a celebrity speaker to your school. Think about the celebrity you would choose to have speak; then, write a letter to persuade your principal to invite this person. Be sure to include convincing reasons and details to support your choice.

....

....

....

....

....

....

....

....

....

....

....

....

....

....

It has been said that television has little real educational value. What is your opinion on this issue? Write an essay stating your opinion and supporting it with convincing reasons. Be sure to explain your reasons in detail.

....

....

....

....

....

....

....

....

....

....

....

....

....

....

Girls and boys often enjoy playing the same sport. Some people believe that girls and boys should be able to play on the same team. What is your opinion on this issue? Write an essay stating your opinion and supporting it with convincing reasons. Be sure to explain your reasons in detail.

....

....

....

....

....

....

....

....

....

....

....

....

....

....

NARRATIVE

Think about a time when something unexpected happened. Write a story in which you tell about an unexpected event that happened to you or someone you know.

....

....

....

....

....

....

....

....

....

....

....

....

....

....

....

....

You have made a very important discovery – one that will make you famous throughout the world. Write a story in which you tell about your discovery and how you made it. Be sure to include details about the setting and any characters in the story, and be sure that your story has a beginning, a middle, and an end.

Think of your best day in school. What happened that makes this day stand out in your memory? Write a story for a friend that tells about what happened on this day in school.

....

....

....

....

....

....

....

....

....

....

....

....

....

....

....

....

....

Talk about a time you felt disappointed. Include what you expected from the situation and how reality did not live up to your expectations.

....

....

....

....

....

....

....

....

....

....

....

....

....

....

....

....

It is often said that animals are humans' best friend. Describe a time in your life when this saying proved to be true.

....

....

....

....

....

....

....

....

....

....

....

....

....

....

....

....

....

Martin Luther King Jr. said that he wished for the day when his children "would be judged not by the color of their skin but by the content of their character." Write about a time in your life when the content of your character was tested.

....

....

....

....

....

....

....

....

....

....

....

....

....

....

....

People often say "Don't judge a book by its cover." Describe a time when you misjudged someone based on his or her appearance or when someone misjudged you.

....

....

....

....

....

....

....

....

....

....

....

....

....

....

....

....

Sometimes lies can have serious consequences. Describe a time when a lie had major consequences for you.

....

....

....

....

....

....

....

....

....

....

....

....

....

....

....

....

....

Parents are our first and most important teachers. Describe a time when you learned a valuable lesson from one of your parents.

....

....

....

....

....

....

....

....

....

....

....

....

....

....

....

....

We often discover something we didn't know about ourselves (or others) when we are forced to handle an unexpected situation. Describe a time when you were faced with something unexpected and what you learned in the process.

....

....

....

....

....

....

....

....

....

....

....

....

....

....

....

....

It isn't always easy to do what is right, and sometimes it can even be dangerous. Describe a time when you put yourself at risk (physically, socially, emotionally, or professionally) to do what you thought was right.

....

....

....

....

....

....

....

....

....

....

....

....

....

....

....

....

....

Some of our most memorable moments are when we achieve an important goal. Tell about a time when you accomplished a goal you had been working toward.

....

....

....

....

....

....

....

....

....

....

....

....

....

....

....

....

....

Write a story about a scientist who discovers a new planet.

....

....

....

....

....

....

....

....

....

....

....

....

....

....

....

....

....

You has the opportunity to go on the adventure of a lifetime and you have to choose between Italy, Hawaii, or Thailand for your upcoming vacation. Write a short story about your adventure

....

....

....

....

....

....

....

....

....

....

....

....

....

....

....

....

Write a story about a snowstorm that shuts down the whole town.

....

....

....

....

....

....

....

....

....

....

....

....

....

....

....

....

....

Write a story about a young student who makes it big in the world of professional video games.

....

....

....

....

....

....

....

....

....

....

....

....

....

....

....

....

....

Write a story about a young teen who loses her cell phone and goes on a series of adventures to get it back before her parents find out.

....

....

....

....

....

....

....

....

....

....

....

....

....

....

....

....

Write a story about a truly unforgettable birthday party.

....

....

....

....

....

....

....

....

....

....

....

....

....

....

....

....

Write a story about two friends who reconnect after many years apart.

....

....

....

....

....

....

....

....

....

....

....

....

....

....

....

....

....

You fall through a crack caused by an earthquake and find yourself in a highly civilized underworld. Write a story about this world.

....

....

....

....

....

....

....

....

....

....

....

....

....

....

....

....

IMAGINATIVE

If you found a treasure chest buried in your garden, what would you most like to discover inside?

....

....

....

....

....

....

....

....

....

....

....

....

....

....

....

....

Invent an imaginary sport. What are the rules? How does the scoring work? Who typically plays it?

....

....

....

....

....

....

....

....

....

....

....

....

....

....

....

....

....

Imagine that you woke up tomorrow as a member of the opposite sex. What would be different about your life?

....

....

....

....

....

....

....

....

....

....

....

....

....

....

....

If you were invisible for a day, where would you go and what would you do?

....

....

....

....

....

....

....

....

....

....

....

....

....

....

....

....

Think of someone you dislike or someone whose views and values are very different from your own. Now write a diary entry from their perspective, exploring why they see things this way.

....

....

....

....

....

....

....

....

....

....

....

....

....

....

....

....

....

Imagine a future in which we each have a personalized robot servant. What would yours be like? What would it do? What features would it have?

....

....

....

....

....

....

....

....

....

....

....

....

....

....

....

....

If you could live inside any video game, which would you choose? Why?"

....

....

....

....

....

....

....

....

....

....

....

....

....

....

....

....

If you could meet any character from any book (or TV show or film), who would it be? What would you say to them, and what would they say to you?

....

....

....

....

....

....

....

....

....

....

....

....

....

....

....

....

Where would you go, if you could go anywhere in the world? Who would you want to go there with?

....

....

....

....

....

....

....

....

....

....

....

....

....

....

....

....

EXPOSITORY

Explain why you chose the clothes you're wearing today.

....

....

....

....

....

....

....

....

....

....

....

....

....

....

....

....

Write about a role model of yours. Why do you look up to them?

....

....

....

....

....

....

....

....

....

....

....

....

....

....

....

....

Learn about a traffic law in your neighborhood and explain why it's important.

....

....

....

....

....

....

....

....

....

....

....

....

....

....

....

....

Write about something you learned this year. Use as much detail as you can remember.

....

....

....

....

....

....

....

....

....

....

....

....

....

....

....

....

Choose a character from a story or movie. Explain why they made an important choice.

....

....

....

....

....

....

....

....

....

....

....

....

....

....

....

....

Write a news article about an event from your life or the community.

....

....

....

....

....

....

....

....

....

....

....

....

....

....

....

....

Give your best advice to someone who is about to enter middle school.

....

....

....

....

....

....

....

....

....

....

....

....

....

....

....

Choose a moment in your state or country's history and describe the events that led to that event.

....

....

....

....

....

....

....

....

....

....

....

....

....

....

....

....

SCIENCE

Create a new chemical product. What are its properties and what does it do? What elements do you think it would be composed of?

....

....

....

....

....

....

....

....

....

....

....

....

....

....

....

....

Think about the best habitat for your personality. What animals, plants, and weather would your perfect ecosystem have?

....

....

....

....

....

....

....

....

....

....

....

....

....

....

....

What would be the greatest scientific invention that could help the most people? What would it do to help advance human civilization?

....

....

....

....

....

....

....

....

....

....

....

....

....

....

....

....

Write a short interview with a famous scientific figure
from history. Think about what this person
accomplished. What would they say about their
achievements?

....

....

....

....

....

....

....

....

....

....

....

....

....

....

....

Explain how a certain scientific breakthrough has changed lives or the course of history.

....

....

....

....

....

....

....

....

....

....

....

....

....

....

....

....

....

If you had to design a space station on the moon, what would the station contain? What would be needed for survival and what would you place there for the comfort of the inhabitants?

....

....

....

....

....

....

....

....

....

....

....

....

....

....

....

....

3D printers are being used in science to construct models, make artificial limbs, and create robots. Formulate another scientific use for a 3D printer.

....

....

....

....

....

....

....

....

....

....

....

....

....

....

....

....

Analyze your exercise and eating habits. What small changes could you make to have your body run more efficiently?

....

....

....

....

....

....

....

....

....

....

....

....

....

....

....

....

Smart Homes are houses that use automation to run several features in the home electronically or through the internet. How would you modify your home to be a "Smart Home"?

....

....

....

....

....

....

....

....

....

....

....

....

....

....

Interpret this quote in your own words: "The scientific man does not aim at an immediate result. He does not expect that his advanced ideas will be readily taken up. His work is like that of the planter - for the future. His duty is to lay the foundation for those who are to come, and point the way." Nikola Tesla.

....

....

....

....

....

....

....

....

....

....

....

....

....

....

Made in United States
Orlando, FL
02 July 2024

48549583R00061